PRACTICAL TIME MANAGEMENT
How to get more things done in less time

Bradley C. McRae, Ed.D.

Self-Counsel Press
(a division of)
International Self-Counsel Press Ltd.
Vancouver
Toronto   Seattle

Printed in Canada

First edition: February, 1988
Reprinted: August, 1988; August, 1989

Canadian Cataloguing in Publication Data

McRae, Bradley C. (Bradley Collins), 1945-
   Practical time management: how to do more things in less time

   (Self-counsel series)
   ISBN 0-88908-673-7

   1. Time management. I. Title. II. Series.
   HD69.T54M27   1988   646.7   C88-091091-7

Self-Counsel Press
(a division of)
International Self-Counsel Press Ltd.
Head and Editorial Office
1481 Charlotte Road
North Vancouver, British Columbia V7J 1H1

This book is dedicated to the memory of my father, Collins McRae, who first taught me about time management, and to my infant son, Andrew Collins McRae, who is finishing the job.

CONTENTS

LIST OF SAMPLES

LIST OF EXERCISES

INTRODUCTION

There are other books and articles on managing your time, so how is this book different?

Most of the work on time management has a very specific range of interest. It is usually designed for people in business, and it covers topics like when to read your mail, how to set priorities, and how to decrease wasted time in meetings, in interviews, and on the telephone.

All of these are valuable skills. However, they deal with office-related activities. The purpose of this book is to bring time management out of the office and help you apply its principles to other activities and projects that you would like to accomplish in your non-work time.

The techniques explained here are designed to help people in all walks of life use their time more effectively, with a special emphasis on getting those important things done that you want to do outside of the job. For example, do you want to build a house, go back to school, or get into good physical shape? Or are there other ideas you have left on the back burner because you just haven't had the time? This book will help you to choose what you want to do, pick a time when you want to do it, show you how to get it done, and help you feel better about yourself — all at the same time.

The approach of this book differs from most current self-help books. First, the ideas in this book are derived from principles based on scientific research.

Second, many popular psychology books are repetitive. They take 200 pages to say what could easily be said in 50 (wasting a lot of your valuable time), and they leave much of the implementation of the change process up to you. This book does not do that. Special short exercises and simple activities are provided to ensure that the ideas presented can be transferred to your everyday life. Do the exercises as you go along; you will learn a lot about yourself and every new

revelation will add valuable information to your time management plan.

Third, maintenance is stressed. It is one thing to bring about a change; it is another to make that change a permanent part of your life (until you decide otherwise). To that end, many of the exercises and samples in the book have been reproduced in the Appendix. Use them as they are or as a starting point for customizing your own forms. When you lack resolve in your new plan, you may be surprised at how motivating it is to fill in these forms — to put down in black and white why, how, and when you plan to achieve something.

Finally, profiles of a range of people in varying situations are included so you can see how others have used these concepts and principles to get more done in less time.

Congratulations on making the time to read this book, and good luck in developing practical time management skills that will last a lifetime.

1
GETTING MORE THINGS DONE

We all know people who accomplish a great deal in their lives and others who never seem to get anything done. You probably view yourself somewhere in between: happy to be doing a few things on your list, but vaguely wishing you could get to more of what you have been wanting to do for so long.

The major differences between these two broad types of people are their skills in planning projects, their ability to manage their time, and their degree of self-control. If you want to make more of your leisure time, then you need to develop and enhance these skills too.

a. CONTROL AND SELF-ESTEEM

Your abilities in project planning, time management, and self-control are closely related to how you feel about yourself as a person. And how you feel about yourself has something to do with the discrepancy between the way you currently perceive yourself (your self-image) and the person you would like to become (your ideal image). The greater the difference between your self-image and your ideal image, the lower your self-esteem. Likewise, the closer you come to realizing your ideal image—becoming your ideal self—the higher your self-esteem.

One of the main determinants of your self-esteem is the sense of control you have over your time and accomplishments. *You can increase this control.* In turn, this greater control will bring you closer to your ideal self and raise your self-respect. But no book alone can do this for you; you must read the remainder of this book carefully, do the exercises conscientiously, then develop your plans and carry out your projects. The situation is very similar to wanting to play a better game of tennis. You wouldn't just read a book on tennis and let it go at that. You would carefully read it, and then you would go out on the court and try to improve your game by first working on your forehand, then your backhand, your serve, and so forth. Step by step, you would work your way to a stronger game.

In many of the exercises in this book, you are asked to change certain aspects of your behavior and then evaluate the effects of those changes. There is an emphasis on behavior because it is easier to *act* your way into a new way of behaving than to *think* your way into a new way of acting.

What it all boils down to is the use of the scientific method, only in this case you are both the scientist and the experiment. Some scientists work better than others; the good ones take their work seriously.

b. WHERE DOES THE TIME GO?

Exercise #1 is a time survey. It consists of 36 statements that tend to be true of people who use their leisure time effectively. Mark each statement as either true or false, as it applies to you. You should take the test again after you have completed this book to determine how much progress you have made. (There is a blank copy of this time survey included in the Appendix.)

EXERCISE #1
TIME SURVEY

	True	False
General		
I am very satisfied with the way I use my time off the job	☐	☐
It is very important for me to use my time off the job effectively	☐	☐
I make the best use of my time I possibly can	☐	☐
I feel in control of my time	☐	☐
At the end of the day, I feel good about what I have accomplished	☐	☐
I feel certain of whom I am and where I am going	☐	☐
I am willing to take a risk to get the important tasks of the day completed	☐	☐
I seldom find myself wasting time	☐	☐
I work fast and efficiently	☐	☐
Goals and planning		
I schedule my activities several days or weeks in advance	☐	☐
I am able to delegate responsibility to others when appropriate	☐	☐
As I begin the day, I know what I would like to have completed before I go to bed that night	☐	☐
I set short, medium, and long-term goals	☐	☐
I think out and plan the most efficient use of my time	☐	☐
I tend to be systematic in my daily planning	☐	☐
I set goals for myself that will take months or years to reach	☐	☐
It is fun to plan for the future even though the plans may not work out	☐	☐
I organize my daily activities so that there is little confusion	☐	☐
I plan much of my life around a few main goals	☐	☐
I have my future and the route to it well mapped out	☐	☐

	True	False
Time		
I apportion my time so that I can manage each day to do everything I want	❏	❏
I usually plan for some extra time to cover unforeseen events	❏	❏
I find it easy to say "no" to unimportant and meaningless activities	❏	❏
I know my best times for concentration and make good use of them	❏	❏
I work steadily at my own pace	❏	❏
I tend to work according to schedule	❏	❏
I have an accurate idea of how I use my time	❏	❏
I work at my best when I have to meet a deadline	❏	❏
I finish most tasks according to schedule	❏	❏
I meet self-imposed deadlines by beginning and finishing tasks at prearranged times	❏	❏
Self-control		
When I find myself wasting time, I get back on track	❏	❏
I think positively and encourage myself when starting major projects	❏	❏
I quickly recognize when I am procrastinating	❏	❏
I have developed techniques to overcome procrastinating	❏	❏
I get right to work at the jobs that have to be done	❏	❏
I do important tasks first	❏	❏

Total: True_____ False_____

2

DECIDE WHAT YOU WANT TO DO

Most people spend a lot of time thinking about the past and wondering what they want out of the present or future. For the purposes of this book, let's concentrate on the future.

Think of your future as a trip with several possible destinations. For each destination, there are a few likely routes. Without picking a destination and selecting a particular route, you are likely to waste time taking a road that could stop at a dead end or land you at the wrong place at the wrong time. Without a plan you risk attaining your goals too slowly, haphazardly, or not at all.

a. SETTING GOALS

Good goal-setters tend to have a well-developed sense of their future and what they want from it. A clear feeling of what you want means you will be able to take advantage of options and opportunities as they come along.

We often devote more thought to how we will spend our vacations than to how we will live the rest of our lives. We do this because our vacations are important to us: we know we have limited time and we want the holiday to turn out well so we give vacations a high priority. If you devote as much attention to getting things done when you are not on vacation, think of what you can accomplish! Use Exercise #2 to explore your own sense of setting goals.

In addition to the qualities you listed in Exercise #2, there are four important factors in successful goal-setting.

EXERCISE #2
GOAL-SETTING QUALITIES

Take a few minutes to think of someone you know who sets goals.
Then think of a person who hardly ever plans far enough ahead to
shop for the evening meal. Write the name of each person in the
blank space provided and then jot down the qualities or specific
skills that make these two people different.

Goal-setter

Name: _____

Qualities: _____

_____

_____

_____

Non-planner

Name: _____

Qualities: _____

_____

_____

_____

When you have finished listing their qualities, rate yourself on a
scale of one to ten on each of these qualities. How close do you
come to either of your acquaintances?

You

Qualities: ( ) _____

( ) _____

( ) _____

( ) _____

Next, in the parentheses provided, number the qualities in the order
that they are most important to you — those qualities you would
like to develop in yourself.

( ) _____

( ) _____

( ) _____

( ) _____

1. Be specific

Effective time users determine goals that are specific. A good rule of thumb is that the more specific the goal, the easier it is to meet it.

Setting specific goals is a hard skill to develop because most of us *think* we are being specific when we really aren't. For example, if Ralph were to say that his goal is to get into good physical shape, many people would think he is setting an honorable, specific goal for himself. However, Ralph would be far better off setting his goal for physical fitness more specifically: for example, to run a mile and a half three times a week.

2. Be positive

Research has indicated that positive goals are more likely to be met. Instead of setting yourself the task of eliminating a bad habit, translate it into something positive. You can do this by selecting a behavior that is incompatible with the negative behavior. For example, if your goal is to not watch so much television, re-word it that you intend to use that time doing more reading, refinishing furniture, or taking a cooking course instead.

3. Be realistic

The goals you set for yourself should be specific and they should be defined as *what* you will do, *when* you will do it, and *where* you will do it. If you determine the frequency and duration of an action, you are well on your way to making a real change in your life.

For example, to focus on Ralph's goal of getting into shape, a more realistic goal would be to *run a mile and a half* on *Mondays, Wednesdays, and Fridays* during his noon visits to the local YMCA.

4. Be flexible

The final quality important to reaching your goals is flexibility. Building in some allowance for unforeseen events helps to ensure that you will stick to your program and realize your goal. If you make your plans too rigid, you won't be able to stick to them, and you will become discouraged when you can't meet your expectations.

For example, let's consider that Ralph sometimes has morning business meetings scheduled on the same days he goes to the YMCA. Often the meetings run too long to allow him to get to the track to run his mile and a half. He should modify his goal to running the assigned distance on the assigned days with a make-up session on alternate days should he miss a workout.

This type of planning acknowledges the other needs and commitments in Ralph's life; you need to use the same technique.

b. BRAINSTORMING

Top corporations often formulate future directions after a "brainstorming" session. People meet to consider as many possibilities as they can, realizing that being too critical might eliminate options that may turn out to be solutions to their problems.

Approach the following exercises with a similar open attitude. One of the best ways to find solutions to problems is to take seemingly irreconcilable differences and turn them into creative solutions. If you don't like options A or B, brainstorming can help you develop alternatives that will lead you to option C: a creative solution to your problems.

The following brainstorming exercises will help you focus on what your leisure-time goals are and what you want for the future (see Exercises #3 and #4).

The exercises may not seem appropriate for your situation; if you are in doubt, do the exercise anyway to give yourself as many options as possible.

EXERCISE # 3
FOCUS ON YOU

First, examine your goals, whether they are painting the house, learning a foreign language, or embroidering a tablecloth. To start, quickly write down five things you want to accomplish next week. Do the same for the next month, the next year, five years from now, and ten years from now. Remember, this is a tentative list, not a binding contract. The point is to bring you up to date with yourself, and the best way to do that is by checking with yourself periodically on what you want to do.

Next week I want to:

1. _____

2. _____

3. _____

4. _____

5. _____

Next month I want to:

1. _____

2. _____

3. _____

4. _____

5. _____

Next year I want to:

1. _____

2. _____

3. _____

4. _____

5. _____

Five years from now I want to:

1. _____

2. _____

3. _____

4. _____

5. _____

Ten years from now I want to:

1. _____

2. _____

3. _____

4. _____

5. _____

EXERCISE #4
WHAT IS IMPORTANT?

Consider your priorities. What do you consider most important? What makes you get up in the morning? Complete the following sentence five to ten different ways.

1. To exist is to _____

2. To exist is to _____

3. To exist is to _____

4. To exist is to _____

5. To exist is to _____

6. To exist is to _____

7. To exist is to _____

8. To exist is to _____

9. To exist is to _____

10. To exist is to _____

In the space below, rewrite the list so that the response that is most important to you appears first. Continue ranking your responses until you have completed the list. Beside each, note the percentage of your time that you currently devote to it. Finally, in the column provided, note the percentage of your time you would like to devote to each.

Priority   **% of time current**   **% of time ideal**

1. _____   _____   _____

2. _____   _____   _____

3. _____   _____   _____

4. _____   _____   _____

5. _____   _____   _____

6. _____   _____   _____

7. _____   _____   _____

8. _____   _____   _____

9. _____   _____   _____

10. _____   _____   _____

This is how one woman listed her priorities and the time she allocates to each:

		%of time current	% of time ideal
1.	To exist is to read more books	6%	20%*
2.	To exist is to garden	3%	10%
3.	To exist is to do meaningful work	50%	57%
4.	To exist is to have a meaningful relationship with my husband and children	75%	75%
5.	To exist is to finish my degree	0%	20%
6.	To exist is to ski	5%	10%
7.	To exist is to enjoy my friends	10%	10%
8.	To exist is to travel	1%	5%

* Percentages do not add up to 100%, since categories overlap.

Another woman's focus was different. Sandy's top two priorities were to learn more and to do something creative. Unfortunately, her job didn't offer many opportunities in these areas. Instead of trying to find a new job, she decided to look for more satisfaction from her leisure time. She had thought about taking an evening class in creative writing at the local college, but had never gotten around to it. After thinking over her priorities, she decided to sign up. Now she finds she has a place to be creative and is learning a great deal from the feedback of teachers and other students.

Your objective, like Sandy's, is to bring your *actual* time use and your *preferred* time use into better balance. After all, if you want to earn your degree, shouldn't you be spending more time doing that?

How do you bring your actual times and preferred times into balance? To do this, you need more information.

One of the techniques that Abraham Maslow, the father of humanistic psychology, used to help people get in touch with the part of themselves that helped them realize their full potential, was to have them analyze their peak experiences.

During a peak experience, he said, you are closest to your real self. You are giving yourself messages about the person you want to become. One of the best ways to use your peak experiences is to analyze this message and use it to make the experience a permanent part of your life.

For example, when I was at a conference in Banff in the Canadian Rockies, I suddenly realized that I was totally content and happy. It was as if I had a picture of my life the way I would most like it to be. I had found or achieved a perfect balance to meet all my recreational, intellectual, and social needs. I had all of these things in my life before, but I had never achieved so perfect a balance. Use Exercise #5 to help you analyze your peak experiences.

Another helpful exercise is a guided fantasy, which can help you focus on long-term goals. For example, let's look at Mary's guided fantasy. Mary saw a lake. In fact, she saw the lake in all four seasons, surrounded by trees changing colors in the fall, covered with snow and ice in the winter, budding yellow green in the spring, and shifting sultry in the evening during the summer. Mary and her husband Bill had talked about getting a cottage on a lake for some time, but had always dismissed it as too expensive and too much of a hassle commuting back and forth to the city. Mary was surprised at how strong her fantasy was and decided to talk with Bill about possibly renting a cottage for the coming summer. She wanted to try her fantasy on a trial basis and see if that was really what she wanted.

Use Exercise #6 to develop your own guided fantasy.

There are two other ways you can gather information on possible future goals (see Exercises #7 and #8). Both use visual symbols and are likely to give you a different perspective than the previous exercises. You should do at least one of these exercises, though I recommend that you do both.

c. WHAT DOES IT ALL MEAN?

By completing the goal identification exercises in this chapter, you should develop several pictures of your future goals. When the pictures are developed, you can choose the one you like best. By doing these exercises you create several different

EXERCISE #5
PEAK EXPERIENCES

In the space below, write down several of your own peak experiences. The more detail you use, the more you will get out of the exercise.

_____

_____

_____

_____

_____

_____

_____

_____

_____

_____

_____

_____

_____

Now analyze these experiences to look for directives or goals you can establish for yourself. List those directives or goals in the space below. (Read the following example for an illustration.)

Nick is a personnel officer with the armed forces and works with people all day. He lives on the base and is sociable, so he is usually surrounded by friends during his leisure time. A peak experience for him was going camping by himself — communing with nature, being isolated in the wilderness, not having people around to interrupt his thoughts. He says he was able to enjoy a "profound sense of peace and solitude." The directives Nick is giving himself are to spend more time alone, to experience more solitude in his life, and to spend more time observing nature and enjoying the wilderness.

EXERCISE #6
GUIDED DAYDREAM ANALYSIS

Find a comfortable chair in a room that is quiet and free of distractions. Close your eyes and then tense and relax your feet; do the same with your calves, thighs, buttocks, back, chest, neck, shoulders, upper arms, forearms, hands, and face. Next, stretch and relax your mouth. Then take three deep breaths.

Now imagine yourself waking up in the morning five years from now. Try to "see" your surroundings as clearly and in as much detail as possible: what you are wearing, the color of the curtains, if you are alone or with someone else, how the room is furnished, and so on. Then imagine eating breakfast and getting ready for the day. Think through your activities in as much detail as possible, and imagine how you'll spend the rest of the morning. If you are working, whom do you work with? What happens during the coffee break? Are you in the country, or in a medium-sized town or a suburb? Try to identify the place.

Continue this exercise through the rest of your imaginary day until you imagine yourself going to bed that evening. Try to picture everything as specifically as possible. In the space below, write down the important elements of your day: which things in your daydream seem to be very important, which you already have, which are important for you to attain. Write down the goals that are important for you to attain.

_____

_____

_____

_____

_____

_____

_____

_____

_____

_____

EXERCISE #7
DRAWINGS

You will need some plain paper (minimum size 8-1/2" x 11", although you will find a larger paper works better). You will also need a small package of color crayons.

On the first page make a drawing that represents the way your life seems to you at present. The quality of your artwork is of no concern.

On the second sheet of paper make a drawing of the way you would like your life to be. Then explain the drawings to someone you trust.

Having to explain your drawings to someone else will help you articulate your thoughts. When you finish, translate this information into future goals or activities that your drawings have revealed.

EXERCISE #8
COLLAGES

Gather some old magazines, go through them, and cut out pictures that you like. Don't spend time thinking about why you like them, just pick those that are meaningful to you. When you have finished, divide a large piece of paper in half and place both halves flat in front of you. The section on the left will represent your life as you currently see it, and the one on the right will be your life as you would like it. Now paste the pictures that you have cut out onto one of the two sections depending on which they represent. Again, it is best to do this with a friend because it will force you to be more articulate.

You have had practice with the previous exercises in turning your peak experiences, fantasies, and daydreams into goals. You can do the same here, only the clues for the goals you want to attain lie in the pictures you have cut out.

When you have finished, write down the goals that seem to emerge from Exercises #7 and #8 being as specific as possible.

views of your future. Not only will you have alternatives to choose from, but you can also combine different pictures and make a composite goal that suits you best.

Take a few minutes to read the results from each exercise and summarize them. What are you saying to yourself? What goals seem to be prominent? What similarities, differences, and inconsistencies are you aware of? The consensus of people who have tried these exercises is that they have been better able to identify and clarify their goals, which was their first step in gaining more control over their lives. And controlling how you spend your time is the ultimate control over your life.

3
HOW DO YOU SPEND YOUR TIME?

If I waste a minute, I waste an hour; if I waste an hour, I waste a day; if I waste a day, I waste a lifetime!

A. Solzhenitsyn, Cancer Ward

One of the major factors controlling how close you are to being the person you would like to be is your skill in managing your time. If you can control how you spend your time, you can control your life. In order to put your time management skills into practice, you need an overall view of how you spend your time. Don't be misled; just because you happen to have had a few fruitful evenings lately, you may believe it is always that way. Likewise, if you've encountered a few snags in getting things done recently, don't be discouraged into thinking that it will always be that way. Looking at the whole picture will help you see how close you come to spending your time in the way you would like.

a. THE WHOLE PICTURE

The following exercise will help you see the whole picture by categorizing your time and illustrating that how you actually spend your time may differ from how you want to spend it. Do Exercise #9 now.

b. MONITORING YOUR TIME USE

How you spend your time says a lot about what is important to you, just as how you spend your money says a great deal. If you wanted to know if you were spending your money in a manner consistent with your priorities, you would probably prepare a budget and keep track of expenses. Do the same with your time. Like a money budget, this may not be

Step #1:

This exercise will help you develop categories to use in identifying how you spend your time. Examples of these are —

Work

Household maintenance

Relaxing

Miscellaneous

Play

Recreation

Friends

In the space below, list the categories that fit your lifestyle:

1. _____

2. _____

3. _____

4. _____

5. _____

6. _____

7. _____

8. _____

9. _____

10. _____

Step #2:

Divide the first circle on the next page into wedges reflecting how you currently use your time using as many time categories as you need. Do the same with the second circle reflecting how you would like to use your time.

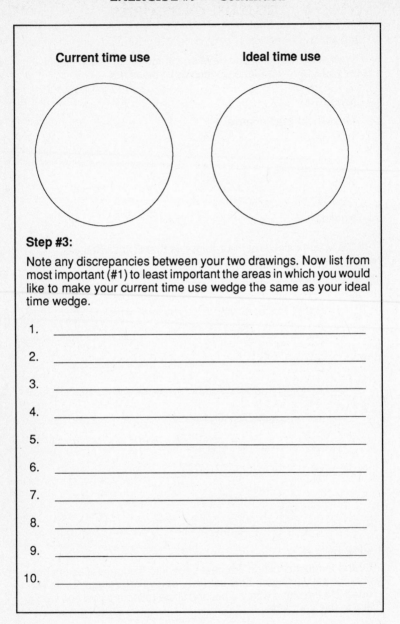

Current time use　　　　　　**Ideal time use**

Step #3:

Note any discrepancies between your two drawings. Now list from most important (#1) to least important the areas in which you would like to make your current time use wedge the same as your ideal time wedge.

1. _____

2. _____

3. _____

4. _____

5. _____

6. _____

7. _____

8. _____

9. _____

10. _____

something you want to do all of the time, but it is a good exercise to go through at least once a year.

Why do you need a formal system? Because people are not very good observers of their own behavior. In fact, they tend to be quite unreliable! One of the best examples of this is a classic experiment in which a psychologist asked a group of people who wanted to lose weight to write down everything they had eaten during the previous two days. They were then fed only those foods for the next two days, and they all lost weight! Obviously, they had not noted everything they had eaten.

To become a more systematic observer of your own behavior, you need to develop a record-keeping system. This is one of the preliminary steps in bringing about change, and it is called "gathering baseline data." It is important for two reasons. First, it is from this information that you will determine if you are spending your time the way you want. Second, after you have made more effective and efficient use of your time, you will be able to assess your improvement. For example, Alice, a graduate nursing student, was feeling guilty about not spending more time with her family. She felt that she was constantly pulled between her family and her work. When she analyzed her time, she was amazed to discover how much time she spent talking to her friends. Alice decided to tell her friends that since she would be preoccupied with her family and school work, she would have little time for socializing until the end of the summer when she would complete the requirements for her degree. She was then able to reorganize her commitments to be consistent with her priorities. Without knowing precisely what was taking up her time — without collecting baseline data — she would not have been able to do this.

To begin, keep track of how you use your time for one typical week that reflects both weekday and weekend routines. Be careful not to take your data during an atypical week — for example when you have out-of-town guests, are involved in an unusual project, or have to work overtime.

There are two systems described on the following pages that you could use to collect the information: the 24-hour schedule (my system of shared, private, work, and project time); and Learning International's "Managing Time and Territory Program." Try either method, or use a combination of the two. Only by charting an accurate record of your time will you be able to see if you are spending it in a manner consistent with your priorities. (Read through sections 1. and 2. below, choose which you want to use, and then record your time use in Exercise #11.)

1. The 24-hour schedule

Divide your time into the categories below and note the actual time spent at each on the schedule in Excercise #10. When you finish, you will find that there is a certain amount of time that never varies: for sleeping, doing regular household chores, and so on. You won't be changing this time very much, but rather will analyze the variable times described below.

(a) **Shared time** This is the time you set aside for being with others who mean a lot to you: wife, husband, boyfriend, girlfriend, children, and so on. After entering these times on the schedule, circle them with a red pencil and total the number of hours you spend this way.

(b) **Private time** This is the time you set aside to do your own thing: working out at the gym, having a special night out with friends, reading, etc. Circle these times with a green pencil and add up the number of hours spent.

(c) **Work time** This is the time you spend working at all aspects of your job, whether the job is outside the home or housework. Circle this time with a blue pencil and add up the number of hours.

(d) **Project time** This is the time you spend on projects such as home improvements, crafts, evening classes, sports, and so on. Circle these times in black and total the number of hours spent this way.

2. Managing Time and Territory Program*

With this system, by Learning International, you develop your time log by using a kitchen timer or digital watch. Set the timer for 30 minutes. When the timer rings, reset it for 30 minutes and immediately write down what you were doing when it went off. This ensures that you have an accurate log of your activities. Although this procedure may seem awkward at first, remember you only have to do it for one week, and it will give you a very specific record of your time.

In the 24-hour system, described earlier, you looked at time in terms of work, shared, private, and project times. Here, you classify your behavior as follows:

(a) *: This is any behavior that helps you move toward your goal.

(b) *n*: This is any behavior that you consider a necessary evil, like doing housework or grocery shopping.

(c) *e*: This is any behavior you choose as an elective — that is, a discretionary behavior such as going for a walk, learning a new sport, and so on.

After you have crossed off all your work time and sleep time, you can figure out what percentage of your remaining time is devoted to *, *n*, and *e* behaviors. Your goal, then, is to reduce, transform, or eliminate *n* behaviors and to develop a balance between the * and the *e* behaviors.

3. Summary

After you collect the data, by whichever method, put it into summary form. You will be surprised to see both the exact number of hours you spend in various activities as well as the relative proportions of time you devote to them. Then look specifically at the activities that make up these categories. Are you using your time in a manner that is consistent with your

EXERCISE #10
TIME USE SCHEDULE

Use either the the 24-hour schedule method or the "Managing Time and Territory Program" to fill in this chart. Complete instructions are provided on pages 21 and 22.

Week of _____

Hour	Sun.	Mon.	Tues.	Wed.	Thurs.	Fri.	Sat.
7:00							
7:30							
8:00							
8:30							
9:00							
9:30							
10:00							
10:30							
11:00							
11:30							
12:00							
12:30							
1:00							
1:30							
2:00							

EXERCISE #10 — Continued

Hour	Sun.	Mon.	Tues.	Wed.	Thurs.	Fri.	Sat.
2:30							
3:00							
3:30							
4:00							
4:30							
5:00							
5:30							
6:00							
6:30							
7:00							
7:30							
8:00							
8:30							
9:00							
9:30							
10:00							
10:30							
11:00							
11:30							

priorities? (A blank Time Use Schedule is included in the Appendix if you want to do this exercise again, later.)

c. SCHEDULING YOUR TIME

You can also use a time log to develop an effective schedule. A scheduled activity is much more likely to occur than an unscheduled one. For example, joggers who have a regular place and time to run are much more likely to carry out a training program than those who do not.

After you get used to your schedule, it will become habit, and habit reduces start-up time and procrastination. Having a definite stopping time also helps. If you know that you will stop in 30 minutes, your task will seem more manageable, and it will be easier for you to get started.

Your schedule should also include regular breaks. As noted in *Coping With the Load* by S. Hodson and P. MacFarlane (Dalhousie University, 1979), "most people get their best work done by working intensely for a reasonable period of time, then resting or changing to something else. There is an optimum cycle of work for every job and every individual." Experiment to discover the work/break cycle that allows you to work most effectively.

You can also organize your schedule to take advantage of your "prime times." We know that people work more effectively at different times during the day. Coordinating prime times with important activities is to your advantage.

Effective scheduling should allow you to gradually increase your performance level to where you feel comfortable with the task but can still see improvement in the amount that you do. The idea of increasing performance by successive approximations is called "shaping." This idea was expressed by D.L. Watson and R.G. Tharp in their book *Self-Directed Behavior*: "There are two simple rules for shaping: (1) you can never begin too low, and (2) the steps upward can never be too small. Whenever you are in doubt, begin at a lower level or reduce the size of the steps. This has the effect of making it easy to perform the desired behavior." Therefore, you should begin working at a level that will ensure success and raise your sights slowly.

28

Finally, when you stop working, stop completely. End all thought of the one more thing you could have done. If you have a good idea, write it down and pursue it later. Tell yourself that you are off duty now and will resume work at your next scheduled work period. Then relax actively — that is, do something that is so interesting or demanding that you cannot think of your previous project at the same time.

Remember that this is only the beginning of your time plan, and you will make some changes in it as you go along. In the weeks to come modify your plan if your needs change. The idea is to develop a balance among the times you spend with others, with your work, engaged in your projects, and by yourself.

d. PLANNING TIME WITH OTHERS

One of the most common problems that couples face in a relationship is controlling their time. We've already discussed making a time log for yourself. If you are married or in another couple relationship, you may find it useful to ask your partner to fill out a time log also to develop a flexible plan that allows both of you to make effective use of your time.

e. TRY IT OUT

Use the time scheduling sheet in Exercise #11 to outline your time for the coming week. Be specific, but remember that the plan is tentative and should be flexible.

If you were to use your baseline data to set up a tentative three-week schedule, what would that plan look like? What projects would you work on? Where and when would you work? Set reasonable, time-limited goals that gradually increase results (shaping), and schedule the work that requires most concentration during your prime times. Make a detailed outline of these components in Exercise #12. Think about some of the steps you will be taking to ensure that your time is used more effectively. What have you learned from compiling the baseline data and how has it changed your life? (Extra copies of the Time Scheduling Sheet and the Three-week Planning Sheet are included in the Appendix.)

EXERCISE #11
TIME SCHEDULING SHEET

Week of _____

Hour	Sun.	Mon.	Tues.	Wed.	Thurs.	Fri.	Sat.
7:00							
7:30							
8:00							
8:30							
9:00							
9:30							
10:00							
10:30							
11:00							
11:30							
12:00							
12:30							
1:00							
1:30							
2:00							
2:30							

EXERCISE #11 — Continued

Hour	Sun.	Mon.	Tues.	Wed.	Thurs.	Fri.	Sat.
3:00							
3:30							
4:00							
4:30							
5:00							
5:30							
6:00							
6:30							
7:00							
7:30							
8:00							
8:30							
9:00							
9:30							
10:00							
10:30							
11:00							
11:30							

31

EXERCISE #12
THREE-WEEK PLANNING SHEET

Month_____

Sunday	Monday	Tuesday

Wednesday	Thursday	Friday	Saturday

4

OVERCOMING INERTIA

You can make all the schedules you want, but if you don't follow through on them you will never succeed in managing your time or your life. In the previous chapters, we have discussed how to set your priorities and how to schedule your time. Now you must determine if it will all work. If you have been honest with yourself in assessing your time, you need only carry through with your plans. But is there still something stopping you? Are you procrastinating?

a. GETTING THINGS DONE

Procrastination is a major time killer. In her book, *The Ann Landers Encyclopedia A to Z*, Ann Landers notes that "most of us equate delay with plain old-fashioned laziness. But in my experience, much true procrastination is not the fruit of sheer sloth so much as it is of indecisiveness born of fear or uncertainty of outcome. Another cause is ignorance or confusion about how to set about doing what needs to be done."

Ann Landers is right on the mark. People put off doing things because they need a sense of what is important, they don't have the necessary skills, they lack confidence, or they wish to avoid the unpleasant. Most of us procrastinate and then compound the situation by berating ourselves for doing so. Procrastination only grows. If you put off doing one thing you don't want to do, then chances are you will put off others until your schedule is in pieces.

Perhaps the hardest part of curing procrastination is seeing through your own excuses. In 1987, I completed a survey on the excuses people use to procrastinate. Some of the most common ones follow. Do you recognize yourself?

"I don't know how to do this."

"In general, I like to put everything off until tomorrow."

"I'm too tired."

"I procrastinate mainly by doing various household jobs that need doing sometime, but not right now."

"Tomorrow I'll start and when tomorrow comes, it's again...well, tomorrow is soon enough."

"I make a list containing too many things to get done in the allotted time and just don't get to those I dislike or am having trouble getting started at."

"I don't have time to do this."

"I always look at the time and feel that there certainly is more time than I need for a project so I can do something else first."

"I'm too busy with day-to-day work to get any projects done later."

"I tell myself I need food or sleep to be able to do something. Then I tell myself I can't work on a full stomach."

"I usually need a break, even when I haven't worked on anything."

"I can't work in a cluttered atmosphere, so I clean up instead of doing what I should be doing."

"Baseball and hockey games are only on television two seasons, so I can't miss them."

These are just some of the comments people make to rationalize not doing what they had planned. Perhaps you have made these statements yourself. Look at your excuses and determine if you are merely procrastinating. Discover what is stopping you from completing a task and then try to overcome that. For example, you may be delaying because you lack certain information: obtain it so you need not wait any longer. You may be procrastinating because you can't make up your mind about something: consider all your alternatives and make your decision. You may be hesitating because you don't know how to take a calculated risk: determine what your potential gains and losses might be and take the plunge.

Look at the procrastination survey in Exercise #13. Think back to the last time you postponed doing something and decide whether you *really* had to wait. Write down the excuse you used then. Consider other times you delayed starting a project, and jot down your rationalizations for hesitating. Look over these comments, and see how many were justified. Were you procrastinating?

b. GETTING MOVING

If you have hesitated — procrastinated — for some very good reason, then perhaps you need to examine your time schedule or your goals. Perhaps you have set overly ambitious goals for yourself. Maybe you took on too big a project all at once without breaking it down into its component parts or planned your day with too many activities. You need to be realistic in scheduling your activities; allow for flexibility and unexpected changes in plans.

1. Set specific goals

A general goal is hard to meet. Be specific, and you'll accomplish your task. You'll also find it easier to begin and be less inclined to delay.

2. Talk it out

Talk to someone about what you wish to do. By telling a friend and discussing ways to go about it, you will gain a clearer picture of your goal. You will also find that once you have heard yourself, you'll recognize your rationalizations and will gain insight into organizing your task.

3. Get more information

Read about what you want to do if this is the first time you have attempted it. If you are building a fence, buy a book on the subject so you know how to order equipment, mark the lines, and set in the materials. Or ask others who have done similar things; get the advice of your neighbors. Guard against the tendency of spending so much time gathering information that you procrastinate actually doing the job.

EXERCISE #13
PROCRASTINATION SURVEY

In the space below, write down your usual means of procrastination. It may help if you think of specific projects you worked on in the past and what excuses or reasons you found to put off starting or completing them.

PROJECT	REASON FOR DELAY

Determine at what point you have enough information and get started.

4. Make instant tasks

Coax yourself into doing something. Use a small, time-limited activity to get you going. For example, if you have to write a report for a local service group, put down the first sentence, even if it isn't completely the way you want it. That first step breaks the ice; it is easier to go from that point on.

5. Start with the pleasant parts first

The important thing is to get started. If you have trouble doing that, take the task apart and select one aspect that is more pleasant than some of the others. Doing something will inspire you to continue with the remainder.

6. Do it with someone else

Some jobs are simply more enjoyable if you do them with a friend. For example, it may be faster and more fun if you and a friend get together to paint your house. Many quilts would never have been made if it weren't for quilting bees, for example. Or have a friend sand that antique rocking chair so that you can paint it.

7. Set time-limited goals

Parkinson's Law states that work expands to fill the time available for its completion. If you have six hours to complete a task, you will stretch out the work to take all those hours, even though under other circumstances you might have needed only four hours. The efficient person tries to limit the amount of time allocated for each task. By setting a finishing time, you help your efficiency in two ways: the set time period will limit the amount of time you can procrastinate; and the limited period will force you to work more efficiently during that time.

Let's consider an example. Most recently, my goal was to write this book. When I was to start, I found myself spending a great deal of time procrastinating. I wasn't sure I could do it, I didn't know if I knew enough, there was a lot of material on time management, and I didn't know if I had anything new or different to say. Then I would spend hours in the library reading about time management or working on other projects that I had going or thought I was interested in. By the afternoon, I was too tired to write. However, I worried about not writing 24 hours a day, and I rarely got anything else done either. I set up a program for myself where I allocated three hours each morning to working on the book, and all my activity during that time had to relate to the project. Then, finally, I began to write the book.

Parkinson's Law particularly applies to housework. Shirley Conran, in her book *Superwoman in Action*, notes that "[housework] expands to fill the time available plus half an hour: so it is obviously never finished. The important thing is not to do the housework but to decide how much time you are going to allow for [it]. What doesn't get done in time is left undone (perhaps for next time, perhaps forever)."

Don't get caught up in the maze of obligatory chores such as housework. If you strive for perfection and try to complete a task that is basically open-ended anyway, the amount of time you spend doing it will only increase, and you won't be using your time efficiently.

8. Give yourself choices

Take two activities that you equally don't want to do, and give yourself the choice of doing one or the other. For example, Joe didn't feel like putting the snow tires on the car; it was already cold and seemed like a miserable job. He also didn't want to clean out the garage, but he made a deal with himself that one particular Saturday he had to do one or the other. Having the choice between the two things gave Joe at least a sense of freedom. You can make your choice, too, and your chores will seem less onerous.

9. Make your jobs seem fun

Write down the chores on little pieces of paper that you and your spouse have to do, and put them into a jar. Each Saturday have a draw to see who gets what chores to do. The element of chance makes it fun and again takes away some of the burden. By making your tasks more fun, you'll avoid procrastinating. And by sharing the chores, you'll get them done faster and with less hassle.

10. Use a list

Many busy executives keep a "to do" list at work because they find it the best way to get things done. Your Time Scheduling Sheet is one type of list, but you may find it useful to keep shorter, day-to-day lists of things to do. You'll find you will get to doing the items on your list sooner and they will take less time to do, since you'll be doing them more efficiently.

11. Reward yourself

For years industry has used incentives to help increase employee productivity. Psychologists have also known for a long time that if a person wants to increase the frequency of a particular behavior, it is best to reward that behavior. You can use the same principles to make yourself do what you want to do.

There are two main reward systems that you can use: a daily reward — that is, some reward for each time you perform the desired behavior, or put in the desired amount of time — and a final reward for after you have completed your project. For example, Keith wanted to get into better physical shape. His daily reward for exercising was a sauna after he worked out at the gym. If he kept to his program and exercised three times a week for a month, he could have the new gym outfit he wanted. He found that monitoring his behavior — that is, keeping track of the number of times he exercised and looking at the accumulated tallies and thinking of the reward of the new gym outfit — helped him stick to his program. By the end of the month, exercising had become part of Keith's routine, and the reward of feeling physically good was enough to maintain that routine, but his program helped him to make the start and overcome his inertia.

For your program, think of rewards that you can use to help yourself get started. Set up both daily and final rewards. It is also important to note that the value of a particular reward may change in the course of time. Take these factors into account, and come up with a new reward when necessary.

Although this method may sound simplistic, it works — and works well. Try it the next time you have a goal. Keith's

SAMPLE #1
REWARD SHEET

Project	REWARD	
	Daily	Final
Exercising	Sauna	Gym outfit

reward sheet is shown as an example in Sample #1. (A blank reward sheet is provided in the Appendix for your use.)

12. Punish yourself

Under the right circumstances, self-punishment can be very effective in overcoming inertia. With this method, you take something away or forfeit a pleasure if you fail to perform a task you had planned on doing.

Peter was a staunch supporter of a major political party, and he strongly disliked the leader of the opponent party. Peter also had a very important project to complete — his final paper for his university degree. He asked a friend to act as his banker, and then he made out a series of post-dated checks for the "enemy" party's election campaign. His agreement with his banker friend was that for each week Peter did not meet his quota of work on his paper, the friend would mail out a check to the "enemy" party's headquarters.

The first week Peter did not work on his project and he looked on in agony as the check was mailed. The second week he did some work but still fell short of his quota. Even though he promised to make up the work, the check was mailed; there was no provision for make-up (only legitimate sickness), as stipulated in the agreement. The third week Peter fulfilled his quota. The same was true for the fourth and fifth weeks. By now working on his project had become his natural activity, and getting the paper finished had become its own reward. The agreement was terminated.

If you opt for this type of arrangement, remember that self-punishment only works as a deterrent; the trick is to make the penalty so harsh that it is seldom applies. And if you find that your self-punishment program is not working, consider modifying your plan because your quotas may be unrealistic.

13. Make a written contract

In the previous example, Peter had to make an agreement with a friend. A similar plan is to have a written contract with yourself. The written contract serves as a reminder, especially if you keep it in a strategic place. If you want to lose weight, for example, place your contract on the refrigerator door. If you want to cut down on the amount of television you watch, place it near the TV. Sample #2 illustrates this kind of contract. (A blank contract is provided in the Appendix for your use.)

SAMPLE #2
PERSONAL CONTRACT

I, ___Hellen Smith___ , do solemnly swear on this __10th__ day of

June , 198-, to spend __one__ hour(s)/day(s), __constructing my__

__garden shed___ , from __5:00 p.m.__ to __6:00 p.m.__ , __four__ out of

__seven__ day(s)/week(s) per week/month for the next __three__

week(s)/month(s).

Signed: _Hellen Smith_

Witnessed: _J. C. Ewe_

14. Chart your progress

For some projects, you'll have a hard time sticking through to the end unless you have some feedback or see some progress along the way. If the project does not provide such signals, then you need to establish them yourself. Keep track of the time you spend by marking it down on a chart. Over time your chart will give you a visual summary of your progress and a boost to your sense of accomplishment.

15. Go public

If you want to really increase your chances of success, make your project known to others. The encouragement you'll receive from friends and the social pressure you'll feel to continue will be great motivators. Post your chart where friends and family members can watch your improvement.

5
PLANNING TO FINISH

Every moment spent planning saves three or four in execution.

Crawford Greenewalt, former President of
E. I. du Pont de Nemours and Company

Trying to complete a complex task without having a plan is like attempting to build a house without a blueprint. It will take you a lot longer, and you could make some costly mistakes in the process. Not having a plan can present personal problems as well. A good plan can help you develop a sense of mastery and allow you to accomplish more in less time.

Good project planning is no accident, and using the proper skills and techniques will ensure that attaining your goal is no accident either. In this chapter, you will become familiar with the problem-solving sequence, creative solutions, goal-attainment scaling, cost/benefit analysis, force field analysis, and the program evaluation review technique (PERT). You may not use all of these planning aids all the time, but as you come to know them and develop your expertise, you will be able to pick the right method for your next task.

a. GETTING FROM A TO B

In chapter 2, you learned to state your goals in specific and positive terms. Having stated your goal, you need to develop a plan to achieve it. To describe the following techniques, we'll call your starting point A and your goal B. The purpose of your plan is to move you from A to B as quickly and easily as possible.

1. The problem-solving sequence

The problem-solving sequence is widely used because it is so easy. This method of planning involves seven steps:

(a) List your goal (point B).

(b) Define your current situation (point A).

(c) Brainstorm possible ways to get from A to B.

(d) Choose one way.

(e) Define the way you have chosen.

(f) Put that into practice.

(g) Evaluate how well you did. (Did you actually reach B?)

For example, Tom had just retired from his job in downtown Toronto (A). For several years he had been troubled by a moderate case of emphysema, and his doctor suggested that he and his wife, Florence, consider the possibility of moving to a warmer climate (B). After a brainstorming session, Tom and Florence decided that they wanted to stay as close as possible to their friends and family. They also decided that since they did not want to make a permanent move, they would rent a house for a year in an appropriate place to allow them to get to know the new area, to see if they felt comfortable there and to develop a sense of community before making any permanent changes. Together, after looking at many alternatives, they picked a location and rented accommodation. Somewhat sadly, but with the spirit of adventure that still characterized their lives, they moved south.

Florence and Tom decided after a year that they weren't happy in their new environment. They felt that they had given it a fair trial, and even though it was better for their physical health, it was better for their mental health to move back where they could be closer to their friends and family all year long.

What you are doing — like Tom and Florence — is systematically setting a goal and planning a way to achieve it. Along the way you may want to continue to strive toward your goal using your original plan, to modify that plan, to try another route, or to abandon your goal.

One student from my time management clinic used the problem-solving sequence very successfully. Susan worked for a company where being bilingual would have helped her advance her career. At the time she had been studying French for five years and was feeling very discouraged. She was taking courses at the university during her lunch hours, while attending conversational courses one evening per week at a private French language tutoring school. Yet she had not reached her goal: she had not advanced in her job.

The problem was not that Susan wasn't making progress; it was that she had ill-defined criteria for success and was heading in too many directions at one time. She didn't have an objective measure of what constituted "being bilingual." What Susan needed was better defined criteria for inter-mediate levels of success and a clearly defined route to reach those goals.

Susan took her problem to the head of the French depart-ment, which she discovered had developed four criteria for language mastery: oral expression, oral comprehension, reading comprehension, and written expression. Susan looked over the criteria and decided that in terms of her career objectives it would be best to improve her oral expres-sion.

The head of the department listened to Susan's oral ex-pression and decided that she was at level 4. Then, together, they came up with a plan to help Susan get from level 4 to level 5: Susan was to take a total immersion course at univer-sity. The course had a good reputation and it would be less costly than taking a similar program in France. By being in-volved with the language every day in a concentrated way, Susan also found that her interest in learning French was rejuvenated, and she returned home and began reading French newspapers and books. By keeping up her French conversation and talking with French friends, Susan soon developed the fluency she needed to be promoted at her job and to develop her knowledge of the language.

2. Creative solutions

Often it can be hard to decide between two alternatives, and you can spend a great deal of time considering first one and then the other, and still not be able to decide. It can help to add a third alternative made up of elements of the two original choices. That third alternative may help you look at the problem from a different perspective.

A creative solution helped Debbie and Mark plan their vacation. One year they decided they would like to visit California. Debbie had visions of seeing San Francisco, eating in good restaurants, and staying in nice hotels. Mark imagined camping in the mountains, visiting the vineyards, and hiking along the coast.

They decided that a third alternative would be best: they would drive to California and camp along the way. They would also allow several days in San Francisco for sightseeing, eating out, and staying in one of the nicer hotels. The third alternative — a creative solution — made both of them happy; neither had to sacrifice their happiness, and both felt they were getting the vacation they wanted.

3. Goal-attainment scaling

Another technique to attain what you want is goal-attainment scaling. One of the reasons we fail to attain our goals is that we don't state those goals in specific enough terms. Another reason is that we don't specify the intermediate steps.

In goal-attainment scaling, you must define your A and B points as specifically as possible. Then pick out points A1, A2, and A3 as your intermediate goals and define these as specifically as possible.

For example, Mike and Shelley wanted to put in a large garden, but they were plagued by big plans and little motivation. Neither knew much about gardening, and both were still feeling tired from their move to their new house and all the work of settling in.

I suggested they try goal-attainment scaling and plan to have the final garden completed in two or even three years.

They could divide the project into a series of five steps and be satisfied carrying out only the first step the first year. They said they immediately felt relieved because they wanted to have a garden but really didn't want to do it all at once and hadn't perceived any alternative.

Mike and Shelley decided they wanted space for both flowers and vegetables in their yard. The first year, they would plant one vegetable bed and one flower bed and seed the rest with grass. Each subsequent year they would add from two to four beds by taking out some of the grass until their garden was the size they wanted. At the same time, they would be building their gardening expertise and be less likely to make costly mistakes. They left the session both motivated and relieved.

Goal-attainment scaling is valuable because it forces you to think out intermediate, manageable steps which make it more likely that you will achieve that goal. Goal-attainment scaling is also a good motivator. It provides you with intermediate goals that are closer and easier to reach. You will feel satisfied along the way; there is no need to wait for all the reward at the end.

Although the standard approach is a five-step system, if you have a complicated project, you may want to use more intermediate steps. Or you may want to use a more complex system known as PERT, which is discussed later in this chapter.

4. Cost/benefit analysis

If your family decided to take a trip from Halifax to Vancouver, you might discuss several ways of getting there. You could drive, take a train, or fly. To help you decide, use a tool many large corporations employ: cost/benefit analysis.

Cost/benefit analysis is a technique to help you balance the cost of something against its benefits. You look at all the factors involved, then compare them in terms of their value. Here is how it works using an example of a cross-country trip.

For a family of four — two adults and two children under 13 — the airfare would be approximately $4,650 for a regular flight (or about $2,872 on a seat sale), plus the cost of getting to and from the airport. The flight takes an average of 6-1/2 hours, and the advantages of flying are that it is fast, convenient, and safe. Of course you don't see as much of the country and you might have to rent a car to sightsee outside the city.

If your family decided to take the train one way, with sleeping accommodations the fare would be around $1,730. In addition, it would cost about $50 a day to eat on the train (or $200 for the entire four-day trip), bringing the total expenses by train to $1,932. You could see more of the countryside, and the trip would be relaxing, but sleeping on a train can be noisy and crowded and, again, to sightsee outside of the city you would have to rent a car.

Your family must decide how important each of the advantages and disadvantages are for each mode of travel and weigh them against the costs of each. The wisdom of your choice depends on how well you collect the facts you need — the costs involved — and how well you assess what is important — the pros and cons of each way of traveling.

For another example, consider the situation that Christine and John found themselves in. Their landlord decided to sell the house they were renting, which meant that Christine and John had three months to find a new place to live. They agreed that they wanted to buy a house instead of paying more rent, but they disagreed on the kind of house they wanted. John hoped to buy an old house and save money by fixing it up. Christine wanted a newer house with minimal upkeep. Both were firm in what they wanted, so they worked it out using a cost/benefit analysis.

	Old house	New house
Cost of house	$ 93,000	$120,000
Taxes/year	1,100	1,346
Lawyer's fees	650	750
Wallpaper, paint, & minor repairs	2,100	–
Roof repairs	2,000	–
Sand floors	850	–
Contingency fund	2,000	1,000
Total	$101,700	123,096

49

The results of the analysis clearly showed that Christine and John could save money by buying an old house and fixing it up themselves. However, the time spent upgrading the house would mean that they would have less free time. The deciding factor, however, was Christine's desire to go back to school part-time and get her M.B.A. There was no way she could work full-time during the day to help pay for the house, take night courses, and paint and repair the house all at the same time. They decided to opt for the newer house with minimal upkeep for the time being and to reconsider buying an older house when Christine finished her degree. The cost/benefit analysis helped them to look at their options more objectively and in greater detail so they could arrive at a decision that fit all their circumstances.

5. Force field analysis

Another reason plans often fail is that all the variables that could influence the plan have not been taken into account. A project planning aid that will help you avoid overlooking such factors is force field analysis. This technique allows you to visualize both the forces driving you toward your goal and those that are working against you to keep you from your goal.

For example, Jane is a homemaker who wants to go back to school. Some of her driving forces are a desire for more intellectual stimulation, a wish to finish a degree that was started years ago, and a hope to develop a career. Some of her restraining forces are having to make arrangements for childcare; negative reactions from her mother, her mother-in-law, and her husband; and the increased work load she'll have from managing both housework and schoolwork.

For problems like this one, there are some strong advantages to using force field analysis. First, it makes you aware of and, therefore, more likely to deal with all the factors that might influence your attaining the goal. Second, it provides three strategies to move you from A to B.

One strategy is to add more driving forces. For example, Jane could find out which courses are available and at what times so she could better coordinate classes with times her children are in school. She could also take a vocational interest test to see how well her interests and career choice match up. It is important to note, however, that when the issues are emotionally loaded, adding more driving forces can backfire because the increased force from the driving side tends to bring about increased forces from the restraining side.

A second strategy is to remove some of the restraining forces. For example, if housework or childcare are restraining forces, Jane could hire a housekeeper or put the children in daycare for several hours while she went to school.

The third strategy is to change a restraining force into a driving force. For example, if Jane's mother or mother-in-law were against her going back to school, she could enlist their aid in watching the children while she took a course. Jane then would have made a solution out of a problem. If you take other people into account in your plans, you have a much greater chance of enlisting their help in reaching your goals.

See Sample #3 for an illustration of Jane's force field analysis. The arrows moving from left to right represent the driving forces that will help move her toward her goal. The arrows moving from right to left are the restraining forces that may keep her from reaching that goal.

SAMPLE #3
FORCE FIELD ANALYSIS

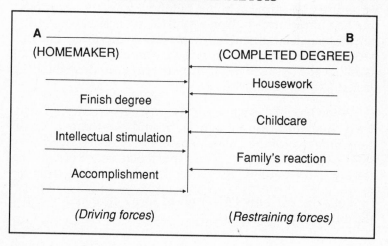

6. Program evaluation review technique (PERT)

The program evaluation review technique, or PERT, was first developed in 1958 by the U.S. Navy. It can be effective in planning any type of project, but it is especially well-suited for large, complex, and lengthy tasks. Many people feel anxious when they undertake a large project because often such projects are vague, open-ended, and ill-defined. You don't have a good idea of the amount of time the project will take, and consequently you don't have a sense of control over your time. PERT is an information gathering device that can give you an accurate idea of the amount of time necessary for the task and allows you to see the end product in terms of the time it will take to achieve it.

The three main components of the PERT process are as follows:

(a) Listing all necessary events

(b) Making time estimates

(c) Developing a PERT flowchart

Don is a traveling salesman with a growing company. His work takes up a great deal of his time, and he is away from home for long periods. This makes it difficult for him to schedule his time and follow a routine. By using the techniques described in this book, he is now able to make much better use of his time at home, but there was still one project that had him stumped. Don was in the process of converting his unfinished basement into a recreation room, den, and furnace room. He started the project over five years ago but hadn't really worked on it in two years; he described the project as a thorn in his side.

When he came to see me, the furnace room was finished. It was July, and Don thought he would like to have everything finished for the holiday season. I suggested that he try PERT, which would give Don a much better idea of what he had left to do and how long it would take him to do it.

Let's discuss how PERT solved Don's problem by looking at its components in depth.

(a) Events

An "event" is a specific, definable accomplishment within a plan, recognizable at a particular point. By listing all the necessary events, you force yourself to begin an analysis of the tasks that lie ahead. Sample #4 shows Don's list of events.

SAMPLE #4
PERT "EVENTS"

PROJECT: Basement

PROJECT EVENTS

1. Put up studding in entire basement
2. Install wiring for lighting and outlets
3. Insulate entire basement
4. Gyprock entire basement
5. Paint two walls in each room and ceiling in recreation room
6. Hang door into recreation room
7. Hang door into the den
8. Put in pine siding on two walls in the recreation room
9. Sand pine siding on the two walls in the recreation room
10. Varnish pine siding on the two walls in the recreation room
11. Put in pine siding on two walls in the den
12. Put in pine ceiling in the den
13. Sand walls and ceiling in the den
14. Varnish walls and ceiling in the den
15. Build in bookshelves in the den
16. Build in desk under the bookshelves in the den
17. Install light and electrical fixtures in both rooms
18. Insulate floors in both rooms
19. Install plywood floors in both rooms
20. Carpet floors in both rooms
21. Contingency event

It is wise to include a "contingency event" in your plan because everyone almost always forgets or overlooks some aspect of a project, or tends to be overly optimistic in estimating the time for getting the various parts of the project completed, or falls victim to Murphy's Law: "If anything can go wrong, it will, usually at the worst possible time." Your contingency event allows some extra time to take care of these things. This way you have built some flexibility into your plan and it is less likely you will be disappointed if everything doesn't (and it won't) go according to schedule.

(b) Time estimates

Action is the means by which an event takes place. Actions represent processes such as putting in the studding or cutting the lumber. For each activity, make three time estimates: a pessimistic estimate, an optimistic estimate, and a realistic estimate.

Your pessimistic estimate assumes that if anything can go wrong it will. For example, Don needed the electrical wiring put in and inspected before he could finish the interior of his rooms, and the electricians went on strike indefinitely. Your optimistic estimate reflects ideal conditions, as if the entire world were arranged to meet your needs. An example of such luck would be if Don needed an obscure piece of plumbing and the local hardware store had the only piece within 100 miles. The realistic estimate usually falls somewhere in between the two. Only with practice will you be able to accurately predict the time you need to do something, and you probably will find it necessary to revise your schedule from time to time. You could also ask experts or friends who have completed similar projects for their estimates of time; ask them for feedback on your project. It is also a good way to get them talking about problems they had. All of this talk will provide you with some valuable advice before you actually get started on your project. Sample #5 shows Don's estimates.

(c) The flowchart

The PERT flowchart is a diagram of events that must occur in order for you to reach your objective. It shows the intermediate steps in a logical sequence as well as their

SAMPLE #5
PERT TIME ESTIMATES

PROJECT: __BASEMENT_____

PROJECT TIME ESTIMATES [1]

		PTE	OTE	RTE
1.	Put up studding in entire basement [2]	8	4	6
2.	Install wiring for lighting and outlets[3]	8	4	6
3.	Insulate entire basement	5	3	4
4.	Gyprock entire basement	14	8	10
5.	Paint two walls in each room and ceiling in recreation room (2 coats)	14	10	12
6.	Hang door into recreation room	2	1/2	1
7.	Hang door into den	2	1/2	1
8.	Put in pine siding on two walls in recreation room	14	10	12
9.	Sand pine siding on the two walls in the recreation room	4	2	3
10.	Varnish pine siding on the two walls in the recreation room	4	2	3
11.	Put in pine siding on two walls in the den	9	7	8
12.	Put in pine ceiling in the den	6	4	5
13.	Sand walls and ceiling in the den	4	2	3
14.	Varnish walls and ceiling in the den	6	4	5
15.	Build in book shelves in the den	5	3	4
16.	Build in desk under the book shelves in the den	5	2	3
17.	Install light and electrical fixtures in both rooms	4	2	3
18.	Insulate floors in both rooms	6	3	4
19.	Plywood floors in both rooms	15	10	8
20.	Carpet floors in both rooms	6	3	4
21.	Contingency event	50	0	12
	TOTAL	191	85	117

PTE = Pessimistic time estimate
OTE = Optimistic time estimate
RTE = Realistic time estimate

[1] Time estimates based on consultation with a friend who had worked in construction. During this conversation Don picked up some valuable construction tips and advice on potential problems.

[2] A carpenter will be hired to help with the studding and the difficult parts of the ceiling.

[3] A friend who is an electrician will help with the wiring.

interdependencies and relationships. This flowchart is critical to the success of your project. It will help you make better use of your time by giving you a feeling for the order you should do things.

Sample #6 shows Don's PERT flowchart for his basement project. Don't be put off by its abstract appearance. The three main paths in the diagram are called critical paths. A critical path is a sequential grouping of related activities. In Don's case these paths are working on the basement as a whole, finishing the recreation room, and finishing the den.

The advantage of having different paths is that if you reach a temporary dead end in one direction, you can move on to other activities. If the electrical fixture Don needs is on order at the store, he could work on the trim in the den instead. Also, with this organization, "a change is as good as a rest:" if you become tired of one task, look at the flowchart and choose a different job.

Don finished his project in time to have a big New Year's party in the recreation room. He says that PERT helped him coordinate the various aspects of the project and fit the project into his hectic work schedule. Don and his family are proud of his accomplishments.

PERT can help motivate you because it will ensure that you divide your work into specific, time-limited tasks that are easier to accomplish than open-ended ones. Using PERT, you will have —

(a) clearer goals,

(b) better task analysis,

(c) more accurate time estimates,

(d) better sequencing of activities,

(e) improved flexibility (differential critical paths),

(f) programmed feedback on progress,

(g) early warning if you are off schedule,

(h) increased efficiency, and

(i) higher motivation.

SAMPLE #6
PERT FLOWCHART

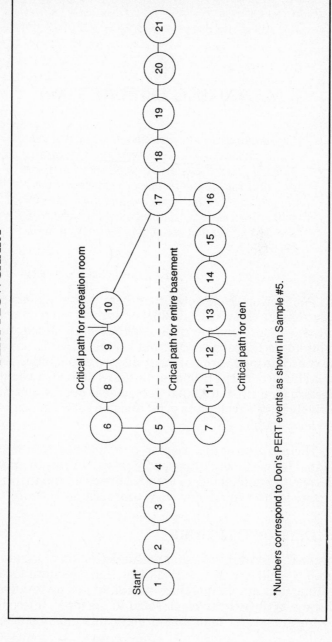

Critical path for recreation room

Crical path for entire basement

Critical path for den

*Numbers correspond to Don's PERT events as shown in Sample #5.

57

6
MANAGING LEISURE TIME

*Old Bureaucrat, my comrade, it is not you who
are to blame. No one ever helped you to escape....
Nobody grasped you by the shoulder while there
was still time. Now the clay of which you were
shaped has dried and hardened, and naught in you
will ever awaken the sleeping musician, the poet,
the astronomer that possibly inhabited you in the
beginning.*

Antoine de Saint Exupery

In 1968, Stewart Wolf noted that there is a relationship between leisure and mental health just as there is a relationship between leisure and physical health. He identified the inability to derive satisfaction from leisure activities as one of the contributing factors in heart disease and sudden death. John Howard, of the School of Business at the University of Western Ontario, found that people who handle tension effectively have developed a good division between work time and leisure time.

The purpose of this chapter is to help you to develop a balance between work time and non-work time, to improve the quantity and quality of your leisure time, and to increase the satisfaction you derive from your leisure.

a. DEFINING LEISURE

I wanted to start this chapter with a definition of leisure, but I didn't realize what a difficult task that was until I started reading through the literature and found that up to one-third of some of those texts are devoted to the topic. Instead, following are several definitions of and quotations about leisure to encourage you to develop a personal definition of what leisure is.

"Leisure is a state of mind." — Old Greek definition

"Leisure is a state of being in which activity is performed for its own sake." — Aristotle

"You can learn more about a person in an hour of play than in a lifetime of conversation." — Plato

"Man does not cease to play because he grows old; man grows old because he ceases to play." — George Bernard Shaw

"Work is whatever a body is obliged to do.... Play is whatever a body is not obliged to do." — Mark Twain

"...There runs a persistent belief that all leisure must be earned by work and good works. And second, while it is enjoyed it must be seen in a context of future work and good works." — Margaret Mead

"Leisure is the portion of time which remains after work and basic requirements for existence have been satisfied." — James F. Murphy

"Lacking an understanding of leisure, many of us become more and more alienated from life and from ourselves." — Alexander Reid Martin

"There was a time when we could sit and listen to our individual, internal rhythms, but now they can hardly be heard over the din of the mechanical clocks set up by school and business and society. Now we have commuting and TV, three-day weekends, and twelve-hour workdays, March migraines and April ulcers, twenty-one-year-old addicts and forty-five-year-old heart attacks." — Dr. George Sheehan

To determine what leisure means to you, complete the leisure survey in Exercise #14.

b. LEISURE ASSESSMENT

To begin assessing the quantity and quality of your leisure time, take another look at Exercise #9 in chapter 3. How close in size are the wedges representing leisure activities in your current time use circle to those in your ideal time use circle? What are you saying to yourself?

EXERCISE #14
LEISURE SURVEY

Just as you previously examined your attitudes toward work, you are now going to examine your attitudes toward leisure. Complete the following sentences as thoroughly a possible.

To play is to _____

_____

_____

To relax is to _____

_____

_____

To be at leisure is to _____

_____

_____

To be at peace is to _____

_____

_____

To experience solitude is to_____

_____

_____

If I were to increase the amount of leisure activities I engage in I would _____

_____

_____

If I were to improve the quality of my leisure time activities I would

_____

_____

60

If you want an accurate idea of how much time you spend on leisure and how much you enjoy the time you spend in various activities, complete the leisure activity log as illustrated in Exercise #15. This may seem an unleisurely activity, but as you probably realize now, your leisure time is a limited and valuable commodity. Wouldn't it be prudent to see if you are spending it wisely?

c. ASSESSING THE QUALITY OF YOUR LEISURE TIME

> We are all of us compelled to read for profit, party for contacts, lunch for contracts, bowl for unity, drive for mileage, gamble for charity, go out for the evening for the greater glory of the municipality and stay home for the weekend to rebuild the house. (Walter Kerr)

One way to assess the quality of your leisure time is through the concepts of "pure" leisure versus "contaminated" leisure. By pure leisure I mean the same thing as Dennis Sparks and W. Furlong when they describe "flow experiences." In his article "The Flow Experience: The Fun in Fun" (*Psychology Today*, 1975, Vol. 10, pp. 35-38.), Furlong wrote —

> Flow experiences are activities that cause individuals to lose all sense of self, time, and the external world. These experiences involve focusing attention on a task that uses one's capacities but does not exceed their limits. Often the flow of experience is accomplished by a sense of ecstasy or contentment....

For example, the other weekend I went whitewater canoeing for the first time. I was completely enthralled with the sport; I felt at one with nature and lost all sense of time and self. When we finished I felt completely refreshed, like I had just come back from a two-week vacation. It is because of the feeling of getting completely outside oneself that, as Dennis Sparks wrote in *Helping Clients Manage Stress: A Practical Approach* (ERIC/CAPS, 1981), "the frequent

EXERCISE #15
LEISURE ACTIVITIY LOG

Date	Leisure activity	Time started/ finished	Number of hours	Who did you do it with? (If by yourself, specify)	Predicted satisfaction (0% - 100%) (to be noted before the activity)	Actual satisfaction (0% - 100%) (to be noted after the activity)

inclusion of flow experiences in a person's lifestyle can be a powerful stress management strategy."

At the other end of the spectrum from pure leisure is contaminated leisure. Contaminated leisure is like the "busman's holiday," where people spend their leisure time doing things closely related to their work, or with the same ferocity as their work. Far too many people take away from the quality of their leisure time in this manner. For example, one of the executives I worked with spent all day at work organizing, controlling, delegating, and writing reports. His main leisure activity was helping to run two charitable organizations. This man was very stressed and his leisure time, instead of being a change from his work, was really the same kind of work in a different setting.

I helped him to identify other activities he would like to do that would provide a refreshing change, but he was reluctant to try them because he didn't know who would run the organizations in his place. I convinced him that it was time to share the responsibility, that he was actually preventing the organization from developing breadth and depth, and that if it were the valuable organization he thought it was, he shouldn't underestimate its ability to take care of itself. He now limits himself to working on one committee for one of the organizations. He has developed other leisure pursuits, such as gardening and spending time with nature, which gives him a complete break from his work. Now at work he find that the is both more productive and significantly less stressed.

I'm not saying that you shouldn't engage in activities that would be considered a busman's holiday. They are a necessary part of life. But if all of your leisure time has some kind of ulterior motive, you could be in trouble.

You can use the concepts of pure and contaminated leisure to help you assess the quality of your own leisure life. Do you need to allow yourself to engage in more "pure" leisure activities? Have you achieved a good balance between the two types of leisure activities described? In the space following, write down three steps you could take to improve the quality of your leisure life.

1._____

2._____

3._____

d. INCREASING THE QUANTITY AND IMPROVING THE QUALITY OF YOUR LEISURE TIME

It is one thing to fill in the leisure survey, another to decide you would like to devote more time to leisure activities and improve the quality of those activities, and yet another to actually carry out those commitments. The exercises in this section are designed to help you do just that.

1. Asserting your right to leisure

Many people feel that they have little, if any, right to leisure. As you grow up you learn to value work in your family and these values are reinforced working in the adult world. Leisure, therefore, becomes not a right but something that you earn after doing so much work. Taken in extremes, workaholics feel guilty, and even become anxious, when they are not working.

Just as some people have to learn to be assertive in social situations (e.g., by sending back a steak that is too rare, by asking the person in the seat behind at the theater to stop talking during the performance, or by asking the boss for that well-deserved raise), other people need to learn to be more assertive with themselves about their right to leisure.

You can learn to be more assertive about this by repeating (and believing) the following statements:

- I have a right to leisure.
- I have worked hard and deserve time off.
- By taking a break, I'll be able to work better.
- Even God rested on the seventh day.

Just as my work can provide me with the opportunity to learn new skills, to develop new friendships, and to satisfy my interests, so can my leisure activities.

This may not be easy, but like all assertiveness training, it gets easier with practice. For example, one Sunday afternoon last fall, Sara planned to work during the afternoon on a report she had taken home from the office. She heard on the radio that the French Concorde had to make an unscheduled landing at the local airport and was very surprised at the battle she had with herself about working versus driving out to see the Concorde. She finally decided that she was being ridiculous — her work wouldn't go away but the Concorde would, and she was able to work better the next day because she took the time off.

2. Thinking up enticing activities

In general, if your goal is to increase the amount of time you spend in leisure activities and to increase the amount of enjoyment you derive from them, you must make your leisure activities enticing enough to carry them out. For example, don't say you would like to go biking; the description is too vague. Say you want to go for a bike ride through the New England countryside on a crisp autumn day after the leaves have started to turn color, and stop at the inn that serves high tea with homemade scones, preserves, and Devon cream. You make the description of the activity so appealing that you will take the time to do it. Use the space below to practice writing an enticing description of your next leisure activity.

_____

_____

_____

_____

3. Leisure activities from the past

Often, for some reason or another, you may find that you are no longer doing many of those leisure activities that you enjoyed in the past. Sometimes this is unavoidable (e.g., you used to ski but no longer live near snow), and sometimes it is not. Complete Exercise #16 to help you look more systematically at the role leisure plays or should play in your life.

EXERCISE #16
REVIVING OLD PASTIMES

List all of the leisure activities that you used to engage in but find you are no longer doing. Then look over your list for those you would like to reintroduce into your life. Place a 1 next to the activity that you would like to do most and a 2 by the next one, and so on.

_____

_____

_____

_____

_____

_____

_____

_____

_____

_____

_____

_____

_____

_____

_____

_____

e. OVERCOMING BARRIERS

In Exercise #16 you were asked to list some of the leisure activities you have done in the past, but are not doing currently, and then to pick out some that you would like to start again. Writing down some of the pleasurable associations connected with these activities will help to increase your motivation as well as the probability that you will once again participate in them. It is also necessary to look at some of the barriers that exist that may keep you from reinstituting your old pastimes.

For example, John identified hiking as one of the activities he would most like to take up again. John grew up on the west coast where he knew where to hike and always had friends to go hiking with. When he moved to the east coast, he didn't know where to go and none of the people he met was interested in hiking. He bought a book on hiking trails, but the book sat on the shelf, and that was the end of that.

When I asked John to identify the barriers that were keeping him from doing what he really wanted to do, he said that he still really didn't know where to hike (reading maps wasn't one of his strong points), and he still didn't know anyone who went hiking. He had heard that the hostelling association in his area had a young adult hiking club, but he hadn't gotten around to looking into it.

He made a commitment to go with the club on their next hike. He found he liked meeting people from different walks of life who had different career interests, and yet had hiking in common. John became an active member and so he was able to revive his old interest in nature. He now feels much more positive about his new environment and is happier about the quality of his life.

Because people move more often now than in the past, it is easy to lose some favorite leisure activities in the process. You must be vigilant to make sure that this doesn't happen to affect your quality of life. One way to prevent it is to identify the barriers that keep you from doing what you want to do, and then, as in the example above, systematically do something about them.

f. THE SOMEDAY PLOY

An easy way to put off your leisure life activities is to use "the someday ploy." You say "someday I'll do this; someday I'll take the time for that." The trouble is that when someday arrives, how will you feel not having done many of the things you wanted to do — even if you accomplished all the work you wanted to. This is the stuff middle-age crises are made of. Exercise #17 should help you realize whether the someday ploy is getting the better of you.

For example, one couple I worked with wanted to buy a home, but had nowhere near enough money to make a down payment. When they asked me how they could start, I suggested they sign up for a course at night school on buying a first home. They took the course and felt better because at least psychologically they were moving closer to their goal.

Another way to get around the someday ploy is to make sure you are as careful about planning and carrying out your leisure projects as you are abut planning and carrying out your projects at work.

Just as people who want to ensure that they read more join book clubs, if you want to make sure you engage in leisure activities, decide you will do at least once a month. For example, my wife and I are going to a resort at the beach one weekend this month and next month a friend and I are going canoe camping.

g. LEISURE RITUALS

Jean and Allan are a dual-career couple, each with high pressure jobs. Shortly after they were married, they took a trip just to get away from it all. Their trip was such a success that they decided to make it an annual event, and throughout the years they have managed to keep it up. Some years, depending on mood and finances, they go to New York City, stay in their favorite hotel, and take in the theater. Other years they stay at a lake resort or go camping. Jean says, "for us it has become an important yearly ritual — no matter what is happening to us in our careers or the current crises with our teenage children." Allan says he looks forward to it every year

EXERCISE #17
OVERCOMING THE SOMEDAY PLOY

List 25 things you would like to do before you die. Then, go over it a second time and mark each activity that is suffering from the someday ploy. Go over it one more time and mark those activities you will start, no matter how small the start is.

	ACTIVITY	SOMEDAY	START
1.			
2.			
3.			
4.			
5.			
6.			
7.			
8.			
9.			
10.			
11.			
12.			
13.			
14.			
15.			
16.			
17.			
18.			
19.			
20.			
21.			
22.			
23.			
24.			
25.			

69

since it gives them a chance to renew themselves as a couple. Establishing your own ritual will add motivation for you to keep up special leisure activities.

h. SOLITUDE

Solitude and the sense of peacefulness that comes from solitude seem to be diminishing commodities in today's world. If you are to experience solitude you must have both the time and the place for it. Once a year my father used to go on retreats sponsored by his church, and I remember being impressed, even as a child, at how rested he was when he came back from those weekends. In the same way, I find a sense of peace in kayaking where no one can make demands on me.

Is solitude important to you? Do you make time for it? Do you have a place for it? If it *is* important for you and you don't have a place and time for it, what are you going to do about it?

Once you have established a time and place for solitude, you must be vigilant and assertive about keeping it. One woman admitted to me that sometimes she likes to go for walks alone, but she senses that her husband feels rejected by this so she always asks him to join her. She has, therefore, lost her opportunity for solitude, although she has never discussed her feelings with her husband.

A man admitted that he built a cottage so he and his wife could "escape." It worked until he start bringing his work with him; then he installed a phone "just to make the occasional call," and now he essentially has three offices: one at work, one at home, and one at the cottage.

The point of these examples is that solitude, like all rare and precious commodities, must be protected. Think carefully about how you can best make your solitude secure.

i. A SPECIAL WORD ABOUT HOBBIES AND VACATIONS

Hobbies and vacations can allow you time to rest, relax, and get a different perspective on things. This section looks at the importance of these activities, and how, if you are not careful, you can undo their beneficial effects.

1. Hobbies

In many areas of life, you often do not see immediate results because there is no simple and direct cause and effect relationship between your efforts and the outcome. Hobbies offer just the opposite. They are usually physical, concrete, tangible activities that give immediate results. For example, Ken, a vice-president of sales, builds model airplanes. He has a card table set up in his living room and often comes home and spends half an hour or so building his models. After working with people all day, he needs a bit of a change. He is then better company than if he hadn't had this brief respite.

While Ken builds his models, Ruth knits, and Chris gardens. Ruth is an editor and after working with ideas all day long, she spends time knitting. She says it gives her the perfect balance to the kind of work she does.

The two activities described above can be engaged in at all times of the year. Gardening is more seasonal, so Chris works indoors during the winter refinishing furniture in the heated basement. But he also continues to plan next year's garden, orders seeds, and starts some of his plants indoors.

Examine what hobbies interest you by completing Exercise #18. One way to get some innovative ideas is to interview your friends and colleagues. New interests make life more exciting and serve as an antidote to stress, so try to keep a balance between the old and the new. For example, one of the things I would like to try the next time it is offered is a course in Chinese cooking.

Once you have selected your hobbies, don't turn them into another form of work like Doreen did. Not only did Doreen spend long hours at work, but she also spent most of her leisure time working as well. So, we made a list of other activities she would like to pursue. Doreen decided to devote more time to painting as it would be a real change from working with people and writing reports. At first she found she felt guilty about not working and had a work-oriented

71

EXERCISE #18
HOBBY LIST

In the space provided, list all of the hobbies you do currently in the first column, then list all the hobbies you would like to try in the second column. Be sure you list hobbies that will cover every season. It is also a good idea to have some hobbies that you can engage in with your spouse and some hobbies that are just for you. Place a "P" next to all the private hobbies and "S" next to the shared ones.

PRESENT HOBBIES
"P" or "S"

HOBBIES TO TRY
"P" or "S"

_____   _____

_____   _____

_____   _____

_____   _____

_____   _____

_____   _____

_____   _____

_____   _____

_____   _____

_____   _____

_____   _____

_____   _____

_____   _____

attitude about her painting — compulsively planning what she was going to do, rushing around to different art supply stores, working long hours without breaks, barely stopping to eat — until the irony of the situation became apparent to her, and she decided to become a more relaxed painter.

2. Vacations

In 1980, *Psychology Today* carried out a survey that provided one of the first comprehensive looks at how North Americans view their vacations. One of the major conclusions was that "for people in extremely stressful jobs, vacations are not a luxury, but may be essential to well-being."

The respondents to the survey reported that vacations allow them to rest, relax, escape routine, and get renewed. More specifically, when the responses where analyzed statistically, the following factors emerged as the main reasons why people take vacations:

(a) Relieving tension: 37% said they need time off to rest, recharge their batteries, and get renewed.

(b) Intellectual enrichment: 18% seek intellectual or spiritual enrichment, to investigate places they have never seen, to discover their roots.

(c) Family togetherness: 13% want to be with their family, to get to know their children better, to visit friends and relatives.

(d) Exotic adventure: 12% seek excitement, exotic adventure, danger, new friends, and sexual escapades on their vacation.

(e) Self-discovery: 11% of vacationers are self-seekers who want to be alone, solve personal problems, and simply enjoy themselves.

(f) Escape: 8% said escaping routine and getting a tan are the most important reasons for taking a vacation.

The respondents also reported that they feel healthier on their holidays. For example, they reported less worry, fewer headaches, less insomnia, etc. There is some indication that vacation can help prevent the emotional exhaustion known as "burn-out."

These are some of the reasons vacations are essential to your well-being, but the quality of your vacations, like the quality of all aspects of your leisure lifestyle, is ultimately your responsibility. You will be able to work better and longer if you look after your other needs as well as you look after your need to achieve and to work.

3. Hints

- Most successful vacationers make a clear division between work time and holiday time.

- Avoid being overly optimistic in what you expect from your vacation (you will only be disappointed).

- Don't turn your vacation into another form of work by trying to do or see too many things; part of the reason for taking a vacation is to escape schedules and deadlines.

- Don't overdo things leading up to the holiday. Ian, for example, is a worrier. Two weeks before his vacation he decided he wanted to get everything done at work before he went away. He started taking fewer breaks than usual and pushed himself to work harder than his usual frantic pace, using the excuse that his vacation wasn't very far away and then he would be able to rest. Ian started his vacation exhausted. It took him the first week to get over being exhausted, and it took him the second week to unwind, so it was not until the time he was ready to go back to work, at the end of the second week, that he was actually ready for a vacation!

j. CONCLUSION

The first step toward achieving a better balance between the value you place on leisure and your actual leisure behavior is to develop a better appreciation of the role leisure plays in your life. I hope this chapter and its exercises have helped you begin doing that.

However, if you still feel that you are not using your leisure time as well as you would like, think about seeing a leisure counselor. They can be found at YM-YWCAs, other community recreational agencies, university departments of recreation, some industrial and business settings, and some mental health facilities.

You have more options than you think, but an option isn't really an option until you know about it. Your leisure counselor can help you assess your interests (or possible interests) by talking with you, or perhaps by administering one of the many leisure interest inventories available.

Once your interests are assessed, your counselor will help you to identify those resources in the community where you can pursue them and encourage and support you so you can carry them out.

As George Sheehan states, the ultimate responsibility is yours:

> As with everything else in life, if you would be educated, you must do it yourself. Heed the inner calling to your own play. Listen if you can to the person you were and are and can be. Then do what you do best and feel best at. Something that gives you security and self-acceptance and a feeling of completion.

7
THE NEW YOU

Now you have some ideas that can carry you through a variety of projects. The application is up to you; time management is a skill that you can use every day in many ways.

Let's take a look at two cases that applied the principles of time management.

a. APPLYING THE PRINCIPLES

Case #1: Bob's house painting project

Bob set a goal of painting the outside of his house by the end of the summer and decided that this was a number-one priority. However, there were a few things in his life that Bob would have rather done. He completed a cost/benefit analysis to look at the cost of hiring someone else to do it, or even hiring a college student to help him, but neither of these options were viable financially.

After completing a PERT chart, Bob realized he could get the house painted if he worked for four hours each Saturday and Sunday morning for five weekends. He decided he would start at 8:00 a.m. and work until noon and that he would take a half hour break between 10:00 a.m. and 10:30 a.m. When he finished he could take a shower and have whatever he wanted for lunch plus a cold beer. He also decided to give himself a reward when he completed the painting — a canoe trip with his best friend over the Labor Day weekend.

What exactly did Bob do? He set up a definite time to start and to stop. He provided himself with a set break, a reward for working each day, and a reward for completing his project. He didn't fight with himself any longer about if and when he should work on his project. This not only avoided emotional wear and tear, but also saved time — the time that used to go into thinking and worrying about his goal was spent actively achieving it. He had a solid plan and felt he was making systematic progress toward it. He also made a clear distinction between his project time and his private time, so he was able to enjoy his private time more; there were no feelings of guilt that he should have been working. When he quit working, he was off duty.

Case #2: Barbara's high school diploma

Barbara had completed all the work for her high school diploma at night school except for the required math course. Barbara hated math; just the thought of doing math made her anxious, but this was her last term and she had to take the math course to get her diploma.

This was an important goal for both Barbara and her husband, Ralph. Ralph agreed that he would do everything he could to help. Barbara decided she would like to study in the morning before Ralph and the children got up. She would get up at 6:30 a.m. and work on her math until 7:30 a.m. while everything was relatively quiet. She and Ralph agreed that he would take over the responsibility for breakfast; all she would do is plug in the coffee.

Unfortunately, Barbara found she couldn't concentrate, even though it was quiet. She spent most of the hour looking at her watch or the clock so she would know when her study time was over so she was available to help with the kids. I suggested that she set the kitchen timer for one hour, and not put her watch on until she finished working. That way she could eliminate the distraction and still know when she put her time in. She agreed to try this for three weeks. By the middle of the second week it was a natural part of her working routine. The distraction was eliminated, and she was working and concentrating better. At the end of the term she had passed her math course and received her high school diploma. Her self-esteem increased, and her family and friends were genuinely proud of her achievement. In fact, her children were so impressed that they began using a timer to help them study and improve their grades as well.

With her new-found confidence Barbara decided that her next project was to find some meaningful part-time work. In an interview, she told a prospective employer about her self-control project. The interviewer was impressed enough with this and Barbara's other skills to offer her the job. One of the spin-offs of this type of project is that Barbara developed learning skills that could be applied in other settings or on other projects. She couldn't lose.

b. KEEPING IT UP

Of course, it is one thing to bring about change and another to maintain that change. You will have to pay particular attention to maintaining the changes that have proved helpful. After working well for a week or so, you may find that you feel sluggish or less productive and are not getting as much accomplished as before. Usually, this occurs after some type of change — for example, after a visit from out-of-town friends; after you finish one project and start another; or after some initial success in your program. You may find yourself using old habits rather than the new techniques, and this calls for a reassessment. The situation is analogous to that of the dieter. Successful dieters make permanent changes in their eating habits. Successful users of time maintain the new habits that have proved helpful. From what you now know about your behavior, what skills will you particularly want to maintain? Write these down as specifically as possible on the maintenance sheet in Exercise #19.

Now that you have identified the skills that you want to maintain, develop a plan to ensure their maintenance. It is a good idea to set up a monthly reassessment schedule — the same idea as having your car tuned up every six months to ensure better performance. Set a specific date, such as the first of each month, to re-evaluate your performance.

There are several advantages to this system. One is that maintenance becomes a built-in part of your program. Another is just knowing that you are going to check your skills will help you stay aware of those aspects of your program that helped you to operate effectively.

EXERCISE #19
MAINTENANCE SHEET

List as specifically as possible the changes you have made that improve your use of time. Then outline the steps that you will take that will ensure that these changes are maintained.

Changes made _____

_____

_____

_____

_____

_____

_____

_____

_____

_____

To maintain these changes I will_____

_____

_____

_____

_____

_____

_____

_____

_____

If, after your assessment, you feel that your performance is not what it could be, reassess your baseline data and reintroduce the appropriate parts of your plan or develop a new one.

Over 100 years ago, the German philosopher Goethe wrote "Knowing is not enough — we must apply. Willing is not enough — we must do!"

This is as true now as it was then, only today we have a better understanding of the psychology of getting things done. This book should help you to use your time more efficiently and effectively and to achieve those goals and greater personal fulfillment. Use it as a workbook, a reference guide, and as a motivator to master practical time management.

APPENDIX
BLANK FORMS FOR MONITORING YOUR PROGRESS

As you have worked through this book, you have been asked to perform certain tasks in various Exercises. Blank sheets are included here for your convenience.

The discussion for each of these exercises is included in the text. The Time Survey is explained in chapter 1. The Time Use Schedule, Time Scheduling Sheet, and the Three-week Planning Sheet are discussed in chapter 3. The Reward Sheet and Personal Contract are used in chapter 4. If you need more copies of these exercises than are provided, you may copy them for your personal use only, at your convenience.

TIME SURVEY

	True	False
General		
I am very satisfied with the way I use my time off the job	☐	☐
It is very important for me to use my time off the job effectively	☐	☐
I make the best use of my time I possibly can	☐	☐
I feel in control of my time	☐	☐
At the end of the day, I feel good about what I have accomplished	☐	☐
I feel certain of whom I am and where I am going	☐	☐
I am willing to take a risk to get the important tasks of the day completed	☐	☐
I seldom find myself wasting time	☐	☐
I work fast and efficiently	☐	☐
Goals and planning		
I schedule my activities several days or weeks in advance	☐	☐
I am able to delegate responsibility to others when appropriate	☐	☐
As I begin the day, I know what I would like to have completed before I go to bed that night	☐	☐
I set short, medium, and long-term goals	☐	☐
I think out and plan the most efficient use of my time	☐	☐
I tend to be systematic in my daily planning	☐	☐
I set goals for myself that will take months or years to reach	☐	☐
It is fun to plan for the future even though the plans may not work out	☐	☐
I organize my daily activities so that there is little confusion	☐	☐
I plan much of my life around a few main goals	☐	☐
I have my future and the route to it well mapped out	☐	☐

	True	False
Time		
I apportion my time so that I can manage each day to do everything I want	☐	☐
I usually plan for some extra time to cover unforeseen events	☐	☐
I find it easy to say "no" to unimportant and meaningless activities	☐	☐
I know my best times for concentration and make good use of them	☐	☐
I work steadily at my own pace	☐	☐
I tend to work according to schedule	☐	☐
I have an accurate idea of how I use my time	☐	☐
I work at my best when I have to meet a deadline	☐	☐
I finish most tasks according to schedule	☐	☐
I meet self-imposed deadlines by beginning and finishing tasks at prearranged times	☐	☐
Self-control		
When I find myself wasting time, I get back on track	☐	☐
I think positively and encourage myself when starting major projects	☐	☐
I quickly recognize when I am procrastinating	☐	☐
I have developed techniques to overcome procrastinating	☐	☐
I get right to work at the jobs that have to be done	☐	☐
I do important tasks first	☐	☐

Total: True_____ False_____

TIME USE SCHEDULE

Use either the the 24-hour schedule method or the "Managing Time and Territory Program" to fill in this chart. Complete instructions are provided on pages 21 and 22.

Week of _____

Hour	Sun.	Mon.	Tues.	Wed.	Thurs.	Fri.	Sat.
7:00							
7:30							
8:00							
8:30							
9:00							
9:30							
10:00							
10:30							
11:00							
11:30							
12:00							
12:30							
1:00							
1:30							
2:00							

Hour	Sun.	Mon.	Tues.	Wed.	Thurs.	Fri.	Sat.
2:30							
3:00							
3:30							
4:00							
4:30							
5:00							
5:30							
6:00							
6:30							
7:00							
7:30							
8:00							
8:30							
9:00							
9:30							
10:00							
10:30							
11:00							
11:30							

TIME USE SCHEDULE

Use either the the 24-hour schedule method or the "Managing Time and Territory Program" to fill in this chart. Complete instructions are provided on pages 21 and 22.

Week of _____

Hour	Sun.	Mon.	Tues.	Wed.	Thurs.	Fri.	Sat.
7:00							
7:30							
8:00							
8:30							
9:00							
9:30							
10:00							
10:30							
11:00							
11:30							
12:00							
12:30							
1:00							
1:30							
2:00							

Hour	Sun.	Mon.	Tues.	Wed.	Thurs.	Fri.	Sat.
2:30							
3:00							
3:30							
4:00							
4:30							
5:00							
5:30							
6:00							
6:30							
7:00							
7:30							
8:00							
8:30							
9:00							
9:30							
10:00							
10:30							
11:00							
11:30							

TIME SCHEDULING SHEET

Week of _____

Hour	Sun.	Mon.	Tues.	Wed.	Thurs.	Fri.	Sat.
7:00							
7:30							
8:00							
8:30							
9:00							
9:30							
10:00							
10:30							
11:00							
11:30							
12:00							
12:30							
1:00							
1:30							
2:00							
2:30							

Hour	Sun.	Mon.	Tues.	Wed.	Thurs.	Fri.	Sat.
3:00							
3:30							
4:00							
4:30							
5:00							
5:30							
6:00							
6:30							
7:00							
7:30							
8:00							
8:30							
9:00							
9:30							
10:00							
10:30							
11:00							
11:30							

TIME SCHEDULING SHEET

Week of _____

Hour	Sun.	Mon.	Tues.	Wed.	Thurs.	Fri.	Sat.
7:00							
7:30							
8:00							
8:30							
9:00							
9:30							
10:00							
10:30							
11:00							
11:30							
12:00							
12:30							
1:00							
1:30							
2:00							
2:30							

Hour	Sun.	Mon.	Tues.	Wed.	Thurs.	Fri.	Sat.
3:00							
3:30							
4:00							
4:30							
5:00							
5:30							
6:00							
6:30							
7:00							
7:30							
8:00							
8:30							
9:00							
9:30							
10:00							
10:30							
11:00							
11:30							

THREE-WEEK PLANNING SHEET

Month_____

Sunday	Monday	Tuesday

Wednesday	Thursday	Friday	Saturday

THREE-WEEK PLANNING SHEET

Month_____

Sunday	Monday	Tuesday

Wednesday	Thursday	Friday	Saturday

REWARD SHEET

| Project | REWARD | |
	Daily	Final

PERSONAL CONTRACT

I, _____, do solemnly swear on this _____ day of

_____, 19___ , to spend _____ hour(s)/day(s),_____

_____ , from _____ to _____, ____ out of

_____ day(s)/week(s) per week/month for the next _____

week(s)/month(s).

Signed: _____

Witnessed: _____

BIBLIOGRAPHY

Bliss, E. C. *Getting Things Done*. New York: Bantam Books, 1976.

Campbell, D. *If You Don't Know Where You Are Going, You'll Probably End Up Somewhere Else*. Niles, Illinois: Argus Communications, 1974.

Conran, B. *Superwoman in Action*. New York: Penguin Books, 1977.

Hodson, S. & P. MacFarlane. *Coping With the Load: A Practical Outline of Effective Study Technique*. Dalhousie University, 1979.

Lakein, A. *How to Get Control of Your Time and Your Life*. New York: Signet Books, 1973.

Landers, A. *The Ann Landers Encyclopedia A to Z*. New York: Ballantine Books, 1978.

LeBoeuf, M. *Working Smart: How to Accomplish More in Half the Time*. New York: Warner Communications Co., 1979.

MacKenzie, R. A. *The Time Trap: How to Get More Done in Less Time*. New York: McCraw-Hill, 1972.

Maslow, A. H. *Toward a Psychology of Being*. (2nd ed.). New York: Van Nostrand Reinhold Co., 1968.

Scott, D. *How to Put More Time in Your Life*. New York: New American Library, 1980.

Solzhenitsyn, A. *Cancer Ward*. New York: Dial Publishing Co., 1968.

Thoresen, C. E. & M.J. Mahoney. *Behavioral Self-control*. New York: Holt, Rinehart & Winston, 1974.

Watson, D. L. & R.G. Tharp. *Self-directed Behavior: Self-modification for Personal Adjustment*. (2nd ed.) Monterey, California: Brooks/Cole Publishing Col, Inc., 1977.

Xerox Learning Systems. *Managing Time and Territory*. Stanford, Connecticut: Xerox Learning Systems, 1974.

CANADIAN
ORDER FORM
SELF-COUNSEL SERIES

PROVINCIAL TITLES

Divorce Guide
❑ B.C. 9.95 ❑ Alberta 9.95 ❑ Saskatchewan 12.95
❑ Manitoba 11.95 ❑ Ontario 12.95

Employer/Employee Rights
❑ B.C. 7.95 ❑ Alberta 6.95 ❑ Ontario 6.95

Incorporation Guide
❑ B.C. 14.95 ❑ Alberta 14.95 ❑ Manitoba/Saskatchewan 12.95 ❑ Ontario 14.95

Landlord/Tenant Rights
❑ B.C. 7.95 ❑ Alberta 6.95 ❑ Ontario 7.95

Marriage & Family Law
❑ B.C. 7.95 ❑ Alberta 8.95 ❑ Ontario 7.95

Probate Guide
❑ B.C. 12.95 ❑ Alberta 10.95 ❑ Ontario 11.95

Real Estate Guide
❑ B.C. 8.95 ❑ Alberta 7.95 ❑ Ontario 8.50

Small Claims Court Guide
❑ B.C. 7.95 ❑ Alberta 7.50 ❑ Ontario 7.50

Wills
❑ B.C. 6.50 ❑ Alberta 6.50 ❑ Ontario 5.95
❑ Wills/Probate Procedure for Manitoba/Saskatchewan 5.95

PACKAGED FORMS

Divorce Forms
❑ B.C 11.95 ❑ Alberta 10.95 ❑ Saskatchewan 12.95
❑ Manitoba 10.95 ❑ Ontario 14.95

Incorporation
❑ B.C 14.95 ❑ Alberta 14.95 ❑ Saskatchewan 14.95
❑ Manitoba 14.95 ❑ Ontario 14.95 ❑ Federal 7.95
❑ Minute Books 17.95
❑ Power of Attorney Kit 9.95

Probate
❑ B.C. Administration 14.95 ❑ B.C. Probate 14.95
❑ Alberta 14.95 ❑ Ontario 15.50
❑ Rental Form Kit (B.C., Alberta, Saskatchewan, Ontario) 4.95
❑ Have You Made Your Will? 5.95
❑ If You Love Me Put It In Writing – Contract Kit 14.95
❑ If You Leave Me Put It In Writing – B.C. Separation Agreement Kit 14.95

Interim Agreement
❑ B.C. 2.50 ❑ Alberta 2.50 ❑ Ontario 2.50

Note: All prices subject to change without notice.
Books are available in book and department stores, or use the order form below.
Please enclose cheque or money order (plus sales tax where applicable) or give
us your MasterCard or Visa number (please include validation and expiry dates).
✂---

(PLEASE PRINT)
Name _____
Address _____
City _____ Province _____
Postal Code _____
❑ Visa/ ❑ MasterCard Number_____
Validation Date_____ Expiry Date _____
If order is under $20.00, add $1.00 for postage and handling.
Please send orders to:
SELF-COUNSEL PRESS
1481 Charlotte Road
North Vancouver, British Columbia   V7J 1H1

❑ Check here for free catalogue.

SELF-COUNSEL PRESS INC.
ORDER FORM

NATIONAL TITLES 04/89

_____	Aids to Independence	11.95
_____	Arrested! Now What?	7.95
_____	Asking Questions	7.95
_____	Assertiveness for Managers	9.95
_____	Basic Accounting	6.95
_____	Be a Better Manager	8.95
_____	Between the Sexes	8.95
_____	Business Etiquette Today	7.95
_____	Business Guide to Effective Speaking	6.95
_____	Business Guide to Profitable Customer Relations	7.95
_____	Business Writing Workbook	9.95
_____	Buying and Selling a Small Business	7.95
_____	Design Your Own Logo	9.95
_____	Entrepreneur's Self-Assessment Guide	9.95
_____	Every Retailer's Guide to Loss Prevention	15.95
_____	Exporting From the United States	12.95
_____	Family Ties That Bind	7.95
_____	Financial Control for the Small Business	6.95
_____	Financial Freedom on $5 a Day	8.95
_____	Fit After Fifty	8.95
_____	Franchising in the U.S.	6.95
_____	Fundraising for Non-profit Groups	5.50
_____	How You Too Can Make a Million in the Mail Order Business (Washington & Oregon)	9.95
_____	Immigrating to Canada	14.95
_____	Immigrating to the U.S.A.	14.95
_____	Keyboarding for Kids	7.95
_____	Learn to Type Fast	11.50
_____	Managing Stress	7.95
_____	Margo Oliver's Cookbook for Seniors	9.95
_____	Marketing Your Product	12.95
_____	Marketing Your Service	12.95
_____	Mobile Retirement Handbook	9.95
_____	Newcomer's Guide to the U.S.A.	12.95
_____	Parent's Guide to Teenagers and Suicide	8.95
_____	Planning for Financial Independence	11.95
_____	Practical Time Management	6.95
_____	Radio Documentary Handbook	8.95
_____	Ready-to-Use Business Forms	9.95
_____	Small Business Guide to Employee Selection	6.95
_____	Start and Run a Profitable Beauty Salon	14.95
_____	Start and Run a Profitable Consulting Business	12.95
_____	Start and Run a Profitable Craft Business	10.95
_____	Start and Run a Profitable Restaurant	10.95
_____	Start and Run a Profitable Retail Business	12.95
_____	Starting a Successful Business on the West Coast	12.95
_____	Taking Care	7.95
_____	Travelwise	7.95
_____	Upper Left-Hand Corner	10.95
_____	Wise and Healthy Living	9.95
_____	Working Couples	5.50

STATE TITLES — WASHINGTON AND OREGON

(Please indicate which state edition is required)

Divorce Guide
❏ Washington (with forms) 12.95   ❏ Oregon 12.95

Employer/Employee Rights
❏ Washington 5.50

Incorporation and Business Guide
❏ Washington 12.95   ❏ Oregon 11.95

Landlord/Tenant Rights
❏ Washington 6.95   ❏ Oregon 6.95

Marriage & Family Law
❏ Washington 7.95   ❏ Oregon 4.95

Probate Guide
❏ Washington 9.95

Real Estate Buying/Selling Guide
❏ Washington 6.95   ❏ Oregon 3.95

Small Claims Court Guide
❏ Washington 4.50

Wills
❏ Washington 6.95   ❏ Oregon 6.95

PACKAGED FORMS

Divorce
❏ Oregon Set A (Petitioner) 14.95
❏ Oregon Set B (Co-petitioners) 12.95
❏ If You Love Me — Put It In Writing 7.95
Incorporation
❏ Washington 12.95   ❏ Oregon 12.95
Probate
❏ Washington 9.95
❏ Rental Form Kit 3.95
❏ Will and Estate Planning Kit 4.95

All prices subject to change without notice.

✂ _

(PLEASE PRINT)

NAME _____

ADDRESS _____

CITY _____

STATE _____

ZIP CODE _____

Check or money order enclosed
If order is under $20, add $2.50 for postage and handling. Allow six weeks for delivery.
Washington residents add 8.1% sales tax.
Please send orders to:

SELF-COUNSEL PRESS INC.
1704 N. State St.
Bellingham, Washington 98225
❏ Check here for free catalog